Mountmellick Work

Jane Houston-Almqvist

Mountmellick Work

IRISH WHITE EMBROIDERY

A survey and manual with full size patterns

Colin Smythe, Gerrards Cross, Buckinghamshire

Mountmellick Work: Irish White Embroidery by Jane Houston-Almqvist is set in Palatino type and printed for the publisher by Redwood Books, Trowbridge, Wiltshire.

Colin Smythe Ltd.
Gerrards Cross
Buckinghamshire
SL9 8XA

Designed by Liam Miller.
Typesetting and page assembly by Design and Art Facilities (Photosetting) Limited, Dublin.
Special photography by Pieterse-Davison International Limited, Dublin.

First published in 1985 by The Dolmen Press.
Published in 1990 by Colin Smythe Ltd.
Second edition 1996, reprinted 2000.

British Library Cataloguing in Publication Data:

Houston-Almqvist, Jane
    Mountmellick work: Irish white embroidery: a survey and
    manual with full size patterns.
    1. White work embroidery
    I. Title
    746.44 TT778.W55

ISBN 0-85105-512-5

Contents

Foreword   *page 7*

Part I   Mountmellick Work: The Background   9
         Fine pieces in collections   15
         Bibliography   22

Part II Mountmellick Work: Technique   25
         Designs   25
         Transferring designs onto fabrics   26
         Materials   26
         Stitches   26
         A leaf sampler to make   33
         A sampler showing twenty leaves   34
         The knitted fringe   36
         Quilts and clothing   37
                                                                 38

Part III Mountmellick Work: Pattern Sheets   39

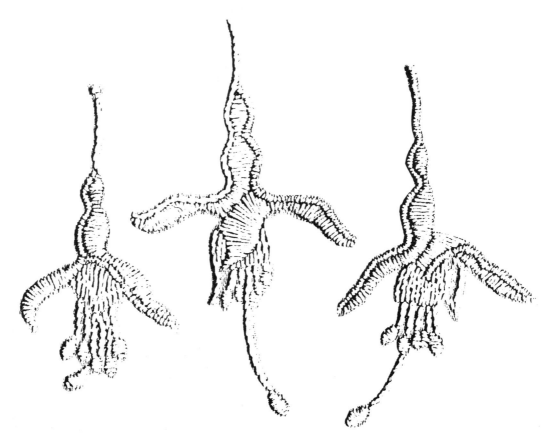

Modern design – fuchsia detail from wedding cushion.

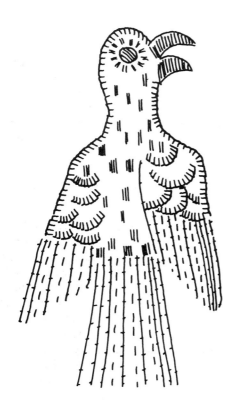

This book is dedicated to
Sister Teresa Margaret McCarthy
and to
Anna E. Wigham
for their love of Mountmellick Embroidery
and for their generous encouragement and assistance
and to
Paddy,
for his love and patience

'Here the needle plies its busy task,
The pattern grows; the well-depicted flow'r,
Wrought patiently into the snowy lawn,
Unfolds its bosom; buds, and leaves, and sprigs,
And curling tendrils, gracefully disposed,
Follow the nimble finger of the fair:
A wreath, that cannot fade, or flow'rs that blow
With most success when all besides decay.'

COWPER

Foreword

'Many and varied will be the recollections of old scholars; but we would
fain hope that each one can find some bright spot on the page of
memory, over which to linger, whether it be the remembrance of long
rambles through lanes and fields to hunt for sweet violets and early
primroses, or the scramble over hedges and ditches to secure the finest
and juciest blackberries, much to the detriment of dress and hands, and
the risk of gaining the soubriquet of "wild injuns." '

Reminiscences of a Mountemellick scholar, 1886

Mountmellick white embroidery – named for the place in Ireland in which it
developed – is deservedly known and recognized by serious embroiderers and
textile historians everywhere as a definite style. As it is all white, its beauty does
not, perhaps, appeal to those who respond to more flamboyant needlework with
lots of colour. It appealed to me very much when I saw my first example in the
late 1960's and I was curious to know more about the town, the country-side and
the conditions which produced Mountmellick embroidery. By chance, a few
years later, I met Sr. Teresa Margaret, who, using a Victorian needlework book,
had taught herself some of the Mountmellick stitches and was very pleased to
share her skills and her knowledge. I discovered that a number of the old
designs were still extant, drawn on brown or greasproof paper or even on
oilcloth. As these designs are still in use by needlepersons eager to learn
Mountmellick white work, there is a danger that the patterns will shortly
disintegrate and be lost to us forever. I also discovered that the old needlework
directions were difficult to find and in some cases difficult to follow when found,
as Victorian engravings tend to show the finished stitch but not steps leading up
to completion. As my mind was tuned into Mountmellick embroidery, I began
to notice that in recent articles and books where Mountmellick work was
mentioned, the accompanying photographs were not of authentic work. Even
worse, a 1982 needlework publication advocated doing this beautiful white
embroidery in coloured thread! So I felt it was time to do some research in order
to satisfy myself and perhaps others. People might be persuaded to look again
into their trunks to see if that cloth Grandmother left really is Mountmellick
embroidery, or to get out their own needles and thimbles and try it for
themselves. I am not alone in hoping that someday we may have a textile
museum in Ireland, where good examples of our rich textile heritage – the
weavings, the laces, the embroideries, patchwork, quilting, knitting – could be on
display and there would be study facilities as well. Perhaps this survey will be
one more brick in the foundation. I would also like to mention an added
personal pleasure which has nothing to do with embroidery; I have become
much more acutely aware of hedgerow and forest growth – the ferns, ivys and
berries – for at its best, Mountmellick embroidery is a glorious tangle of flora
translated into stitchery, a memory of walks which have been and are to come.

I want to thank all the people who have been kind enough to share with me
their knowledge of Mountmellick work and have let me examine and
photograph work they own. In particular, I would like to thank the following:
Olive Abraham, Alexandra College and Jean Hazlett, Eithne Byrne-Costigan,

Foreword

Patricia Donlon, Doreen Foley, Muriel Gahan, Olive Goodbody, Lenore Keane, Annie Kelly, Ada Longfield Leask, Sheena Millington, The Mountmellick Embroidery Group: Betty Dunne and Sr. Teresa Margaret McCarthy, The National Museum of Ireland and Mairaid Reynolds, Cecil O'Donahue, Elinor Robinson, The Religious Society of Friends: Richard S. Harrison and Terence Mallagh, The Royal Dublin Society and Alan Eager, Anna S. Wigham.

The illustrations in this book derive from a variety of sources. The wood engravings are reproduced from Weldon's *Practical Needlework* manuals published in the last century. The photography is by Pieterse Davison International Limited, Dublin, with the exceptions of illustrations 8, 9 and 10 which are reproduced from photographs supplied by the museums in whose collections the pieces are preserved, illustration 11, which is from a photograph by Frank Hunter, and illustrations 5 and 6 which are from my own photographs. I also made the line drawings throughout the book.

Jane Houston-Almqvist
Saint Patrick's Day 1984
Dublin

Part I: Mountmellick Work: The Background

White embroidery of various kinds has been done in Ireland for several centuries: the knotted cord appliqued to a quilt by Mrs. Delaney, friend and contemporary of Dean Swift; the 'flowering' or 'sprigging' done on fine muslin in Ulster, quite like Ayrshire white work. The 19th century saw the development of new styles and techniques, among those Mountmellick embroidery and the two embroidered laces from Limerick and Carrickmacross. A dictionary defines lace as a delicate ornamented network of threads and embroidery is defined as ornamental needlework on a ground. Mountmellick embroidery, stitched on closely-woven white cotton satin 'jean' and with cotton thread also in white, has a subtle richness and great elegance. To aid in identification of Mountmellick work, characteristics of the work are as follows:

It is *always* white-on-white.

Contrast: that of the smooth satin stitch against padded and knotted stitchery, and contrast of the cotton satin fabric with the more matt cotton embroidery thread.

The absence of eyelets or open-work (though the occasional eyelet does appear in a fine example).

Natural floral design, fairly large in scale.

The buttonholed and fringed edges.

1. *A leaf worked in raised satin stitch.*
2. *Pansy in buttonhole stitch and honeycomb.*
3. *Natural forms: A bunch of hops*

The Background

4. Knitted fringe for trimming Mountmellic work.

Though the area was settled many years before, Mountmellick town was founded by Quakers (members of the Society of Friends) in the 17th century. Mountmellick was once a prosperous linen and cotton spinning and milling centre, known as the 'Manchester of Ireland'. In a statistical survey of The Queen's County, 1801, we read: 'Even girls are taught, at so early an age, that literally they are scarcely able to carry home the piece of goods of their own weaving. The process (of having a journeyman weaver teach their children at home) is obviously very simple, and proves the absurdity of serving the seven year apprenticeship to every trade, whether more or less intricate. This insures work within doors, when agriculture cannot be pursued by severity of weather, and affords a double source of income, and a certainty of constant employment. The manufacturer imports the cotton thread, and sometimes buys in Dublin, whither they send all their goods unfinished: from the spinning factory at Mountrath the cotton thread is also had, and the looms are scattered at several miles distance around the town.' However, prosperity declined in the 19th century, with the devastating effects of famine, then political upheavals and changes in industrial techniques. In the town of Mountmellick, as elsewhere around the country, able people worked to aid those less fortunate, and one of these was one Johanna Carter who came upon the idea of introducing a new style of embroidered white work, the sale of which might benefit local women and girls – work which could be done at home and fitted in around other chores. Dates of these beginnings are not exact, but probably Mrs. Carter 'invented' Mountmellick embroidery between 1830 and 1840. She doubtless considered using materials which were easily available and of reasonable cost – perhaps her fabrics and threads were spun or woven in Mountmellick or Mountrath. In any event, she chose to use cotton upon cotton, all in white. The stitches she employed were not unlike those used in other European countries at that time and, as in Jacobean embroidery, a variety of stitches would be used in one piece of work.

Mrs. Carter's 'new' style had a bolder quality than the usual whitework of the period, such as Ayrshire. As well as being able to embroider, Mrs. Carter was also probably an accomplished draftswoman, not unusual in an age when young ladies were taught to sketch and paint. Her design source would have been the profusion of flora along Mountmellick hedges and walls. She had only to leave her door in order to pluck blackberries, wild roses and rose hips, ivy and daisies – her 'models' for the embroidery designs. Even today, there is a charming path along the River Owenass which runs through Mountmellick town; one imagines that Mrs. Carter walked this path many times and noted plants identical to those which grow there still. Mrs. Carter's designs, drawn and embroidered on the 'jean' acquired some popularity at least, and she and her workers were busy for a number of years. About 1847, the Earl of Dunraven (Lord Adare) of Limerick ordered a number of Mountmellick quilts for Adare House. We know that, as 'Carter, J., Mountmellick, Queen's County, Designer and Manufacturer', she exhibited 'embroidered quilt, toilette cover, and doileys' at the Irish Industrial Exhibition in Dublin in 1853. At the same exhibition, the Countess of Eglinton showed 'a quilt richly embroidered in the centre with the Eglinton arms, and worked over with shamrocks, roses, and thistles, designed and executed by Mrs.

5. The path along the River Owenass in Mountmellick

6. Blackberries along the river

Carter of Mountmellick'. The Irish Work Society took a stand at the Great
Exhibition of 1851 in London (the Crystal Palace Exhibition) and among the
exhibits were 'specimens of embroidery, worked *au blanc*, from Midleton
Convent, and Mrs. O'Donovan of Clonakilty'. In 1854, John Sproule edited a
thoughtful paper summing up the 1853 Irish Industrial Exhibition and his views
on contemporary textile cottage industries. In the section on Tapestry, Carpets,
Lace, etc.: 'trade has also been greatly extended through the intervention of
private individuals, who took up the matter more with the benevolent object of
finding employment for the female peasantry around them, than with that of
introducing a branch of trade on any secure basis. In such cases, the degree of
success attained has been in proportion to the energy displayed on the part of
the patrons, and also on the extent to which they had influential connexions
through whom the sale of the produce could be made. An appeal from an
influential lady on behalf of native industry, partaking somewhat of a charitable
nature, and seeking to dispose of articles really beautiful in themselves, was not
likely to be often unsuccessful; and hence some Irish ladies have been able to
obtain high prices for all the work which their dependents could turn out, and so
long as the presiding care which brought matters to this state was continued, all
went right; but even on its temporary cessation great inconvenience cannot fail
to be felt.' The author goes on to mention the necessity for a business-like
approach to both production and marketing, and fears, too, that to be able to
embroider to the exclusion of other simpler needle arts might render the worker
useless to the trade. 'Notwithstanding the large and increasing demand for
sewed muslin and lace, the trade is so dependent upon novelty of patterns and
fashion that periods of reaction are sure to occur in it, unless the greatest activity
and judgment are evinced in catering for the caprice of the consumer. In such
cases, great inconvenience is sustained by the work-people, who may be thereby
thrown out of employment; but this only shows the necessity of the business
being carried on by those who have a sharp eye to profit; as well as the danger of
relying too exclusively on a branch of trade in which casualties are so greatly
felt.' Nevertheless, for one reason or another, girls continued to be taught to
embroider. Between 1850 and 1856, Mrs. Ann Jellicoe, who later founded
Alexandra College in Dublin, directed lace and embroidery schools in Clara, Co.
Offaly, not far from Mountmellick. Some of the designs in this book are from
drawings with the name Jellicoe pencilled on them. There were two Quaker
schools in Mountmellick and young lady boarders were required to embroider
personal necessities, such as nightdress cases and comb and brush bags. Perhaps
the discreet yet bold elegance of this embroidery style appealed especially to the
Quakers, to whom the use of colour would have been regarded as too wordly!
There are many privately owned examples of Mountmellick work, not least
among Quaker families, and it can be substantiated that many pieces were
worked around this area. Eventually the Quaker Mountmellick School building
was bought by Sisters of the Presentation Order who fostered the tradition of
Mountmellick embroidery, teaching it and adding to the collection of designs
which they had been given. And they generously do this still. Thus girls of both
Quaker and Catholic families took their needle skills to other parts of the
country – the Waterford area, the Midlands, Ulster. We do not know when Mrs.
Carter herself stopped working, nor do we know the exact connection, if any,

with any of the schools, but apparently the last of the workers who learned directly from her died about 1870. There seems to have been a lapse in the Mountmellick embroidery cottage industry until a little later in the century. In 1880, a Mrs. Millner started an Industrial Association in Mountmellick in order to help provide a livlihood for 'distressed Irish gentlewomen'. Marketing and sale of the work was most successful – the style of the embroidery again suited the fashion of the times – and by 1890 the Association had about 50 workers. When Alexandra, Princess of Wales, visited Ireland for the second time, in 1885, the Association presented her with a dressing table cover in Mountmellick embroidery. (This was not the only time Mountmellick work was chosen as an important gift: during President Kennedy's 1963 visit to Ireland, he was presented by the National Council of the Blind of Ireland with 'a white quilt for the White House' – a ten by nine foot beauty wth floral and shamrock designs and an unusual deep scalloped border.) Publishers of needlework books responded to the interest and Weldon's, in England, began publishing *Weldon's*

7. A spray of fern from Weldon's Mountmellick Work

Practical Needlework in 1886, and four volumes (booklets) devoted to Mountmellick embroidery were published between 1890 and 1898, which further popularized the work. Altogether Weldon's published eight booklets on the subject, and Wm. Briggs and Co., also in England, produced transfers, as well as instruction booklets of their own. A lady in Belfast stitched samplers of the stitches, which she sold by mail order. So the working of Mountmellick embroidery became more and more a middle-class pastime and less and less a remedy for poverty! To those who did not embroider, sales of finished work were brisk in both Dublin and Belfast and in Cobh, Co. Cork, embroidery was bought by transatlantic passengers who would put ashore for a few hours. In families where laying-out of the dead was practised, bedcovers in Mountmellick – as well as whole sets of special bedlinen – were in use and sometimes shared out to friends and neighbors. The author owns a quilt (from Tipperary) which was primarily used for this purpose. Just as it does today, the Royal Dublin Society continued to encourage the applied arts by sponsoring exhibitions at their premises in Dublin, offering prizes for especially fine work. At the Art Industries Exhibition in 1900, there were 23 entrants from the Midlands and the Dublin area in the Mountmellick work section and a Mrs. Daly of Blackrock, Co. Cork was complimented by the judges on the great variety and good selection of stitches used in her work. The quilts exhibited were not for sale but the average price for a pillow sham or nightdress 'sachet' was 12 to 15 shillings. At the Sheep Show in 1906 there was also a class for Mountmellick embroidery. Again the entrants were from the Dublin area or the Midlands. The top prize was 2 pounds. Among the articles exhibited were pillow shams, cosy covers, children's bibs, frocks, cushions, collars, nightdress bags, toilet covers, brush and comb bags, bedspreads, tea cloths, and tray cloths.

The First World War changed the lives of women in so many ways. Of necessity, many went outside the home to work and when at home, they simplified their lives, as they often found they had to do their own housework, leaving less time for decorative needlework. Fashions for both households and people changed, and for years all these lovely things lay forgotten and unappreciated in boxes in Irish attics. Now, happily, families who own examples of Mountmellick embroidery treasure them as so they should.

Some Fine Pieces of Mountmellick Work

8. Sachet (1880–90)
Victoria and Albert Museum, London.
(The usual edging for Mountmellick work is knitted fringe; the lace edging in this example is not typical.) Stitches: Buttonhole, French knot, crewel, satin, bullion.

9. Coverlet dated 1885 (detail showing date)
The National Museum of Ireland, Dublin. Stitches: Cable plait, bullion, cable, overcasting, crewel, snail-trail, French knot, buttonhole, diamond filling, flake.

10. Dressing table set
The Ulster folk and Transport Museum. Stitches: Indented buttonhole, padded satin, French knot, button knot, buttonhole, running, crewel, single feather.

11. Camisole in heavy cotton satin (worked by the author).
Stitches: Buttonhole, French knot, cable plait, satin, snail-trail.

12. Child's dress and
separate cape
Made about 1889 for the
mother of Rosemary
Rice Furlong.
Gift of Mrs. Furlong to
the Presentation
Convent Collection,
Mountmellick. Stitches:
Padded satin, French
knot, stem (crewel),
feather, Indian filling.

13. Child's Coat with
wide collar.
Made about 1912 for
Doreen Edmundson. It
was made by two elderly
aunts which might
account for the slightly
old-fashioned look of
the little coat.
Edmundson Collection.
Here the embroidered
motifs quite suit the cut of
the garment. The
broderie anglaise was
also hand-done. Stitches:
Snail-trail, detached
chain, padded satin, satin,
bullion, feather, Cretan,
buttonhole.

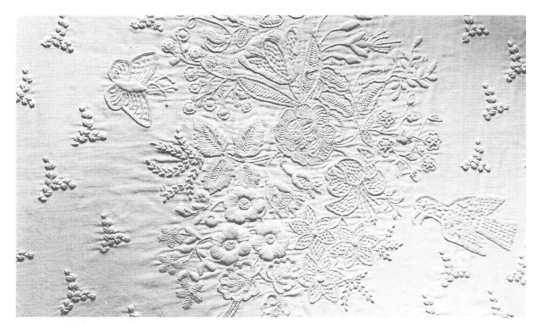

14. Coverlet, centre motif
52" x 48". Gift of the Scully family, Mountmellick, to the Presentation Convent. The rather stiff little bird is a charming addition (and an unusual one!) to this beautifully worked little coverlet. Stitches: Padded overcast, cable plait, bullion, padded satin, feather crewel, French knot, Indian filling.

15. Quilt, centre motif
9' × 9'. Abraham Coll. This quilt was made in the 1870's by E. Abraham who lived in the Slieve Bloom mountains. The quilt is quite large and the scale of the design, the stitching and even the size of thread used are all admirably suited to the size of the quilt. The quilt is stitched on cotton sheeting rather than 'jean'.
Stitches: Indian filling, cable plait, buttonhole, snail-trail, bullion, feather, French knot, stem, cable chain, a few eyelets.

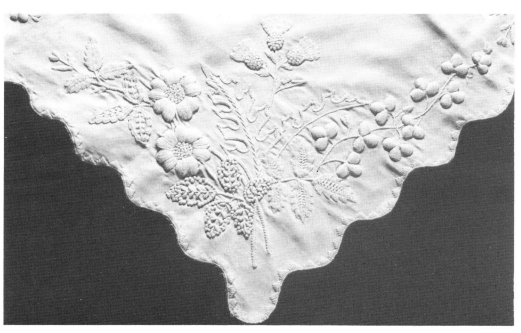

16. Cloth, corner with thistle, shamrock and roses
22.5" x 25". Gertrude Grubb neé Bennis, Waterford (A. Wigham) Note the absence of the fringe. When heavily padded satin stitch is used, it is almost impossible to prevent puckering of the ground fabric. When the rose, the thistle and the shamrock are used together, they symbolize England, Scotland and Ireland. Stitches: Stem, padded satin, cable plait, French knot, bullion, feather, buttonhole, detached chain, Indian filling, feather.

17. Cloth for sideboard (embroidered and fringed on 3 sides only) 50"×29.5". Jacob Collection (A. Wigham)
This cloth has a deep, beautifully worked border with all manner of flora, while the centre is 'powdered' with a pattern of groups of bullion knots. Stitches: Padded satin, bullion, snail-trail, double feather, Cretan.

18. Quilt, border section of Photo 15.
9'×9'. Abraham Collection
Rather than a buttonholed edge, this quilt is finished with an edge of one row of feather stitch between two rows of cable chain. Knitted fringe as usual. Note the boldness of design and stitchery. Stitches: Overcasting, bullion, French knot, Indian filling, cable, cable plait, buttonhole, Cretan, feather.

19. Quilt, centre motif
Coll. Society of Friends, Dublin
An inked label sewn to this magnificent quilt indicates that it was made by Jane Newsom for her son John and his wife Sophia, who were married in 1879 and lived at Templelawn, Cork. The quilt was perhaps a wedding gift. Stitches: Padded satin, overcasting, bullion, French knot, seeding, Indian filling, cable plait, buttonhole, diamond trellis, Cretan, double feather, snail trail.

20. Semi-circular mat 21" x 11". Jacob Collection (A. Wigham) This piece has a particularly clean-cut appearance, due to the very closely worked buttonholing which balances out the heavily padded passion flowers. Stitches: Padded satin, bullion, cable plait, feather, buttonhole, snail-trail, satin, Indian filling.

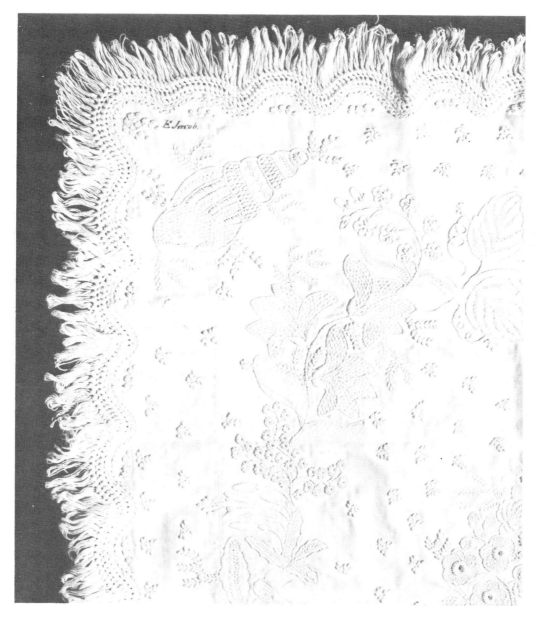

21. Coverlet made in 1879 by Louisa Peet of Tramore for William E. Jacob 44" x 35". Jacob Collection (A. Wigham) The shell motif used here does not occur very often. Note how effectively the simple running stitch is used as a filling, and the berries done in buttonhole wheels encircled by French knots. Stitches: The shell is outlined in cable plait with fillings of bullion, herringbone, running and double feather. Stitches used elsewhere are Cretan, Indian filling, buttonhole, French knot and padded satin.

22. Coverlet, detail of corner. (The centre motif is shown in Illustration 14)
The stylised wheat sheaf appears on all four corners of the coverlet, and the use of filling stitches here is very effective. As well as the harp, the shamrock, thistle and rose appear. It seems apparent that the embroiderer took great delight in doing the stitches and planning just where they should go! Stitches: The shamrocks are worked in three ways – either outlined in cable plait and veined in feather or outlined in French knots or buttonholed. The wheat sheaf is worked in triple feather, diamond filling, cable plait, bullion, seeding, Indian filling. The harp is worked in padded overcast, bullion, feather and stem. The edging is indented buttonhole and two rows of chevron stitch. A detail of another harp from the same coverlet is the cover for this book.

Bibliography

Books, History and Reference

Berry, H. F. *A History of the Royal Dublin Society*. Longmans, Green and Co., London. 1915

Boyle, Elizabeth. *The Irish Flowerers*. Ulster Folk Museum, Belfast. 1971

Crawford, A. & Scott, M. *Mountmellick Pictorial Memories*. Mountmellick Development Assoc., Mountmellick, Co Laois.

Culliton, Tomas, *Legends and Folklore of Mountmellick*. Mountmellick Chamber of Commerce. 1976

Dawson, Barbara. *White Work Embroidery*. B. T. Batsford Ltd. London. 1987

Designs and Patterns for Embroiderers and Craftsmen. ed. M. Nichols. Dover, N. Y. 1974

Feehan, John. *Laois, An Environmental History*. Ballykilcavan Press, Stradbally. 1983

Harbison, Georgiana B. *American Needlework*. Crown Publishers, N.Y. 1938

Killanin & Duignan. *Shell Guide to Ireland*. Ebury Press, London. 1962

Levey, Santina. *Discovering Embroidery of the 19th Century*. Shire Publications, Tring, Herts. (U.K.) 1971

Morris, Barbara. *Victorian Embroidery*. Thomas Nelson & Sons, N.Y. 1962

One Hundred Years of Mountmellick School. Richard Webb & Sons, Dublin. 1886

Orlofsky, Patsy & Myron. *Quilts in America*. McGrath-Hill Book Co., N.Y. 1974

Paine, Sheila. *Chikan Embroidery: The Floral Whitework of India*. (Shire Ethnography) Shire Publications Ltd., Aylesbury, Bucks. (U.K.) 1989

Snook, Barbara. *English Embroidery*. Mills & Boon Ltd., London. 1974

Swain, Margaret. *Ayrshire and Other Whitework* (Shire Album 88). Shire Publications Ltd., Aylesbury, Bucks. (U.K.) 1982

Swift, Gay. *The Batsford Encyclopaedia of Embroidery Techniques*. B. T. Batsford Ltd., London. 1984

Wigham, Maurice J. *The Irish Quakers: A Short History of the Religious Society of Friends in Ireland*. Historical Committee of the Religious Society of Friends in Ireland. 1992

The World Book Encyclopedia, Vol. 14. Chicago. 1963

Books, Stitches

Butler, Anne. *The Batsford Encyclopaedia of Embroidery Stitches*. B. T. Batsford Ltd., London. 1979

Gostelow, Mary. *A World of Embroidery*. Mills & Boon Ltd., London. 1975

Karasz, Mariska. *Adventures in Stitches*. Funk & Wagnalls, N.Y. 1969

Lambert, F. *The Handbook of Needlework*. John Murray, London. 1842

Maher, Maree. *Mountmellick Work: Irish White Embroidery. A Practical Workbook*. Treacymar Publishing Co. 157 Templeogue Road, Terenure, Dublin 6W. 1996

Petersen and Svennås, *Sömmar och Stygn*. ICA-förlaget AB, Västerås, Sweden. 1996

Snook, Barbara. *Embroidery Stitches*. B. T. Batsford Ltd., London. 1970

Thomas, Mary. *Embroidery Book*. Hodder & Stoughton. London. 1981

Thomas, Mary. *Dictionary of Embroidery Stitches*. Hodder & Stoughton, London.

Van Wyck, Hetsie. *Embroider Now*. Perskor Publishers, Johannesburg and Capetown. 1977

Weldon's Encyclopaedia of Needlework (chapter on Mountmellick Embroidery). The Waverly Book Co., London. No date

Wilson, Erica. *Erica Wilson's Embroidery Book*. Faber & Faber, London. 1973

100 Embroidery Stitches. Coats Sewing Group, Glasgow. 1967

Publications & Articles

'Busy Needles', Part 53. Marshall Cavendish Ltd., London. 1982

General View of the Agriculture and Manufactures of the Queen's County. The Dublin Society, Dublin. 1801

Needlecraft Practical Journal: Mountmellick Embroidery. No. 108, 1st Series. Pub.

Bibliography

Wm Briggs & Co., Manchester and London. No date

Quane, Michael. 'The Friends' Provincial School, Mountmellick'. *The Journal of the Royal Society of Antiquaries of Ireland*, Vol. LXXXVIII. 1958

Weldon's Practical Mountmellick Embroidery, 1st, 2nd, 3rd, 4th, 5th, 6th, 7th and 8th Series. Pub. Weldon's Ltd., London. No dates

Catalogues

Official Catalogue of the Great Exhibition of 1851, London. Vol. II

The Irish Industrial Exhibition of 1853. ed. John Sproule. Jas. M. McGlashan, Dublin. 1854

Proceedings of the Royal Dublin Society 1899–1900 (Vol. 136) and *1906–07* (Vol. 143)

Record of the Irish International Exhibition (1902). Hely's Ltd., Dublin. 1909

Irish Bedcovers: Techniques & Traditions. Exhibition mounted Autumn 1981–Spring 1982 by the Ulster Folk and Transport Museum, the National Museum of Ireland and Muckross House, Killarney

Examples of Mountmellick Embroidery may be seen at:

The Religious Society of Friends, Swanbrook House, Morehampton Road, Dublin 4 (by written appointment to the Librarian)

The Embroiderers Guild, Victoria. 170 Wattletree Road, Malvern, Victoria 3144, Australia

The National Museum of Ireland, Kildare Street, Dublin (by appointment)

The Ulster Folk Museum, Cultra Manor, Holywood, Co. Down, N.I (by appointment)

The Muriel Gahan Museum, I.C.A. College An Grianan, Termonfechin, Co. Louth (by appointment)

The Victoria and Albert Museum, Brompton Road, South Kensington, London (by written appointment to the Curator of Textiles)

The Ulster-American Museum, Omagh, Co. Tyrone, N.I. (by appointment)

Spray of orange fruit and blossom. Mountmellick Work design from a page found in the library of an Irish country house. 19th Century.

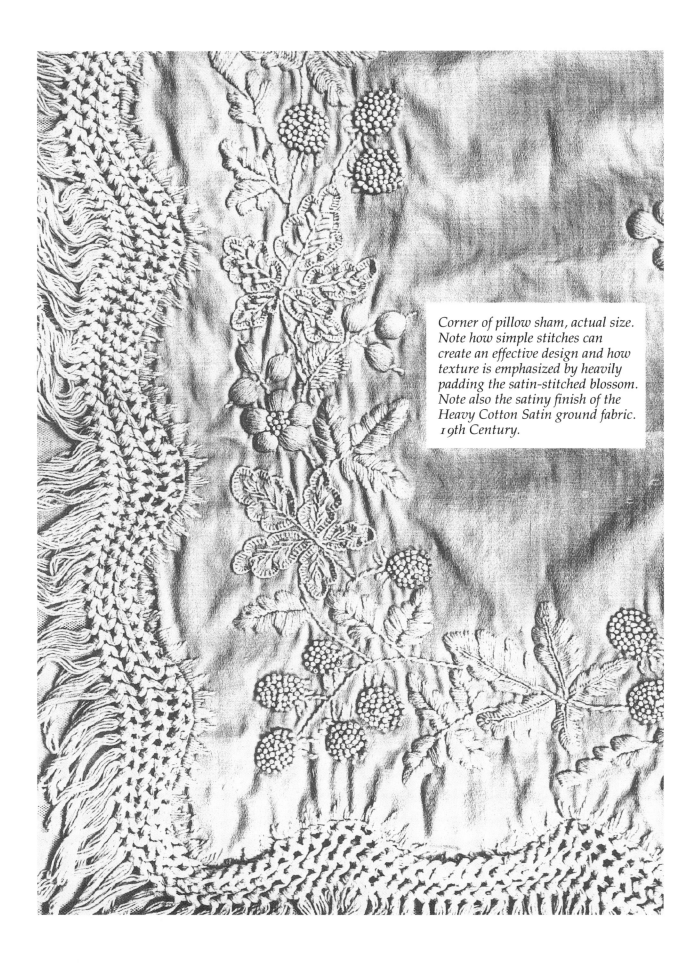

Corner of pillow sham, actual size. Note how simple stitches can create an effective design and how texture is emphasized by heavily padding the satin-stitched blossom. Note also the satiny finish of the Heavy Cotton Satin ground fabric. 19th Century.

Part II: Mountmellick Work. Technique

Designs

The designs included in this book are traced from the original ones in private collections in Ireland. As opposed to the more stylized Jacobean crewel designs, those for Mountmellick embroidery were drawn as realistically as possible – any stylization developed in the stitching. The original designs were usually drawn with one design to a sheet of tissue or brown paper; the designer or amateur embroiderer would make a selection from these drawings for the project at hand arranging them at her discretion over the area to be covered. Weldon's suggested that Briggs' transfer patterns originally prepared for crewel embroidery might well be used 'if only care is taken in selecting such as have a bold, well-defined outline, and plenty of space between the different parts of the design'. The embroiderer was admonished to work with intelligence and keep the whole as true to nature as possible. It was suggested that beginners, whose work might have a tendency to pucker, choose to learn on a small piece: a wild rose, a wheat spray, a spray of ivy leaves or shamrock, a poppy, a Passion flower or perhaps a spray of Forget-Me-Nots. Weldon's also recommended that 'grass may be advantageously combined with almost any flowers, but wheat and barley are appropriate only to be mingled with wild flowers or with garden flowers that bloom in the autumn of the year, such as dahlias, sunflowers, poppies, etc. and would of course be incongruous in combination with lilies, forget-me-nots, or other spring blooming or early summer flowers.' With each new publication on Mountmellick work, Weldon's felt more and more obliged to suggest different uses to which the completed embroidery might be put, as well as 'new' design ideas; if these had been slavishly followed, a weakening of style and purpose would have occured. Articles suggested included children's pelisses, frocks and pinafores, ladies' fancy aprons, panels and borders, using silk threads for the embroidery.

The designs are often quite large in scale – so large, in fact, that if they were worked in colour, the total effect would be garish and vulgar. On fine old pieces of Mountmellick work, the surface is fairly encrusted with embroidery; though the designer of a bedspread might leave quite necessary spaces between clusters of flora, such spaces might be seeded with bullion stitch. The Irish used their own flowers for inspiration. Even the exotic-looking Passion flower is cultivated in Ireland. Legend has it that Saint Patrick plucked a shamrock to demonstrate and explain the Trinity; Victorians liked to see in the Passion flower symbols of the Passion of Christ – the crown of thorns, nails of the Cross, Christ's wounds, spears, whips and swords. It was also doubtless a favourite because it lent itself to rich embroidery treatment – lots of padding and bullion knots.

When choosing designs for your embroidery, remember that smaller designs can be repeated to form an all-over pattern, border or centerpiece. If you are embroidering small mats or placemats, keep the designs away from the centre because of the raised nature of the embroidery. When planning a large project, such as a tablecloth or bedcover, it is a good idea to make tracings of the design elements you want to use, and place these over the fabric until you find a pleasing arrangement.

Try drawing your own designs, using as models the flowers, plants or shells around you.

Transferring designs onto fabric:/

Before transferring the design, *wash and iron* the fabric. This will remove eventual sizing and ensure that it will not shrink. Fix the prepared fabric to a table top right side up with bits of *masking tape* and experimentally move your *tracings* around until you have the placement you want. *Pin* the tracings in place with a pin or two at the top of the tracing. Slip a sheet of *graphite paper* (graphite side down) under the tracing and trace off with a sharpened *hard pencil*. If it is impossible to get graphite paper, use dressmaker's (not office) carbon paper. Remove tracings and pins. Graphite is really powdered pencil lead and will soon brush away, so it is necessary to either keep re-marking the drawings as you embroider, or, preferably, go over the drawing with a *water-erasable pen*. Remember to test the pen first on a scrap of the fabric you are using and to apply no heat, such as an iron, to the ink, otherwise it may not wash out. Never use a biro. Before you start to stitch, it is advisable to machine zig-zag the edges of your fabric.

Materials

It would be pleasant to be able to state that materials for Mountmellick Embroidery are available everywhere, but sadly this is not possible. However, the following suppliers will make every effort to supply the requisite Heavy Cotton Satin ground fabric and the matt (non-shiny) cotton thread.

Fabric: Heavy cotton satin, referred to in older literature as 'jean'. This fabric is satiny on the right side, with plain weave on the wrong side. Heavy cotton satin, in its white state, is usually woven to be sold on to fabric printers for curtain and upholstery fabrics. Examples of Mountmellick Embroidery worked on cotton sheeting or linen are to be found; one assumes that in these cases, the 'jean' was unavailable.

Threads: Traditional Mountmellick Embroidery thread is a *matt* white cotton of the type sold for crochet or knitting rather than embroidery. Mercerized threads have too much sheen to be considered traditional. In the past, there were several weights of cotton thread from which to choose and choice of thread would depend upon the article being embroidered and consequently the scale of the design. Several weights of thread could be used on the same piece of embroidery in order to vary texture in the overall work. The characteristic fringe would be knitted from the same cotton thread, but most often in multiple strands.

Needles: Crewel needles to suit the thread used; the crewel needle has a larger eye than ordinary needles. Straw needles, being long, are useful for bullion knots.

For the knitted fringe: knitting needles #13 (2.25mm) or 14 (2mm).

Technique

Stitches:

A publication from August 1899 (*Mrs. Leach's Practical Fancy Work-Basket*) shows diagrams for twenty-two stitches, enthusing about Mountmellick embroidery but displaying some ambivalance about Ireland itself: 'If the men of England have reason to complain of the weary hours they are obliged to spend trying to disentangle the troublesome skein of Irish politics, the women of England have reason to be grateful for the many pleasant hours in which they can employ themselves profitably and agreeably in the soothing occupation of doing Irish needlework.' Choosing just the correct stitch and working it was apparently just as engrossing then as it is now.

As a characteristic of Mountmellick embroidery is an effect of padded, encrusted bas-relief, stitches chosen are generally those which lie on the surface of the material with as little thread as possible underneath. In modern stitchery books, there are diagrams of 'Mountmellick' or 'Montmellick' Stitch, but earlier sources do not list any stitch by that name. It is one of a number of knotted, braided stitches. Some of the names are delightful, as well as descriptive: 'worms' for Bullion Stitch, Snail-Trail, Coral and Thorn. There are over 40 stitches listed in Briggs' Needlecraft Practical Journal and Weldon's Encyclopedia of Needlework, and even more listed in more recent works. Many stitchers used only a few to great effect, and when they used many, they were careful to maintain unity of design, so that while full of detail, the work as a whole had balance. Many of the stitches are just a variation of a basic one, such as all the buttonhole family. Efforts towards realism were perhaps carried to the extreme in these directions for embroidering bulrushes, which were made of 1/8" of cotton sewn down: 'proceed to stitch each of these tiny lengths quite close together up the centre of the outlined flower until the whole is covered by them. Work the slender tip, or stem, which is at the top of the bulrushes, in a few fine crewel stitches and then proceed to trim the coarse cotton, which is sewn down into shape, using a pair of very sharp scissors. Shape and trim these cottons to the outlined edge, and fray or split the soft cotton scraps a little, so as to get the soft fluffy and rounded appearance of the bulrush, and also to hide the stitching by which it is sewn on.'

Some of the stitches will require considerable practise, such as the Cable Plait Stitch. When studying the stitch diagram, note the position of the thread in relation to the needle and whether the needle enters the material or passes under a thread. It is a good idea to make a stitch sampler, marking a number of parallel and straight lines with your water-erasable pen, as well as circles for filling stitches. You could also add a row of leaves and work each leaf differently, and a small spray of flowers. When stitching, try to avoid the use of knots. It is far better to 'run in' beginnings and endings of threads, taking a tiny Back Stitch as well.

Finished Mountmellick embroidery washes very well but it is best to try to keep it clean while working; wash your hands before stitching and omit using hand creme.

In studying old pieces of work, one learns something of the personality of the worker – some did very fine work and others preferred a bolder more dashing approach. Below is an engraving (from Weldon's) of Blackberry Flowers, Berries and Leaves, next to the line drawing of the same subject, showing the variety of stitches used in the simple shapes.

Blackberry. Working pattern for design below.

Blackberry Flowers, Berries and leaves.
Engraving from **Weldon's** *Practical Mountmellick Embroidery.*

Mountmellick Work Stitches

In Alphabetical order (with alternative names in parentheses).

Bullion Stitch (Worms)

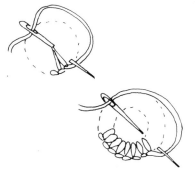

Buttonhole Wheel 1 & 2

Back Stitch

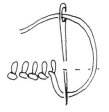

Buttonhole Stitch

Buttonholing, Fringed

Bokhara Couching

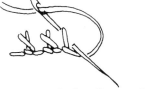

Buttonhole, Crossed

Buttonholing, Indented

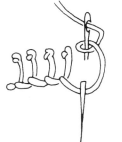

Buttonhole, Knotted

Buttonholing, Sawtooth

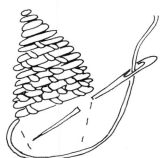

Braid Stitch

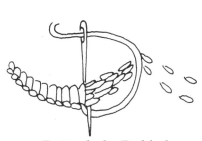

Buttonhole, Padded

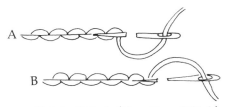

Cable Stitch (Cording Stitch)

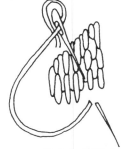

Brick Stitch

Buttonhole, Scallops

Cable Chain

Cable Stitch, Double

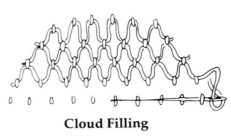

Cloud Filling

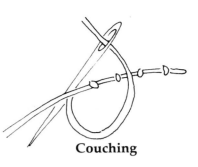

Couching

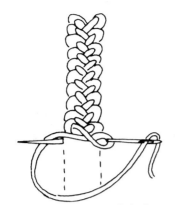

Cable Plait Stitch

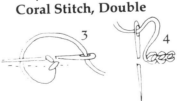

**Coral Stitch, Single
(Knot, Snail-trail)**

Coral Stitch, Single

**Couching, Roumanian (Indian
Filling)**

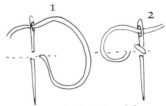

Coral Stitch, Double

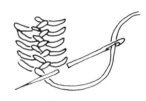

Cretan

Chain, Detached (Lazy Daisy)

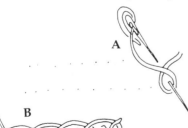

A

B

Chain, Rosette

**Coral Stitch, Double
(Gordian Knot)**

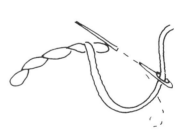

Crewel Stitch (Outline, Stem)

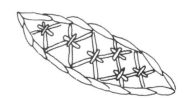

Diamond Stitch & Cross Stitch

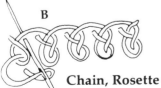

Chain, Twisted

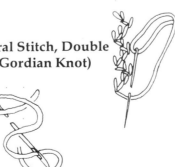

Coral Stitch, Zigzag

Diamond Pattern

Feather Stitch

Fern Stitch

Herringbone

Feather Stitch, Closed

Fishbone Stitch

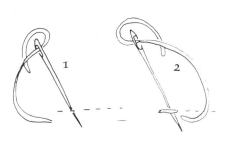

Honeycomb Stitch

Feather Stitch, Double

Flake Stitch

Knot, Double

Feather Stitch, Spanish Knotted

Fly Stitch; Fly Stitch Filling

Leaf Filling

Feather Stitch, Treble

Feather Stitch and Bullion

French Knot

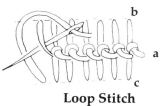

Loop Stitch

31

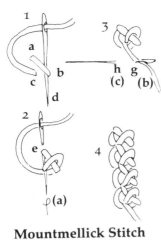

Mountmellick Stitch

Overcast

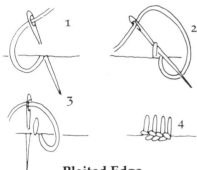

Overcast, Wide

Plaited Edge

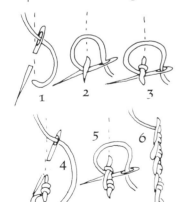

Portuguese Knotted Stem

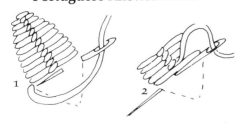

Roumanian Stitch

Running Stitch

Satin Stitch, Flat

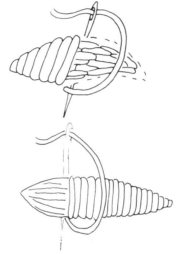

Satin Stitch, Raised or Padded

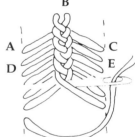

Scroll Stitch

Seeding

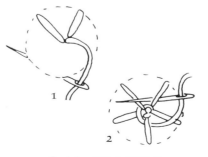

Spider Web Stitch

Stem, Whipped

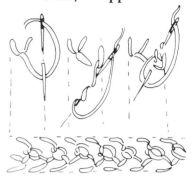

Thorn Stitch

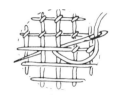

Trellis Stitch

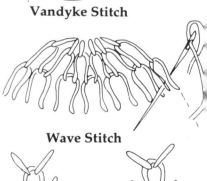

Vandyke Stitch

Wave Stitch

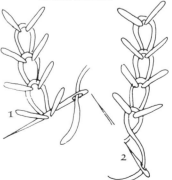

Wheat-Ear Stitch

A leaf sampler

There are many ways to work leaf shapes. Here are some suggestions for working each of the twelve below:

1 outline with SNAIL-TRAIL; vein with FEATHER STITCH

2 slightly padded SATIN STITCH

3 outline in STEM STITCH; vein in DOUBLE FEATHER STITCH

4 work from mid-rib to edge in ROUMANIAN COUCHING, first the right half and then the left. Work stem in CABLE STITCH

5 outline with narrow BUTTONHOLE STITCH. Work mid-rib and stem in CABLE STITCH

6 work in BULLION STITCH, taking the stitches from the centre to the outer edges

7 outline in CABLE STITCH; vein in CHAIN STITCH

8 work right half in SATIN STITCH. For the left half, outline in STEM STITCH and seed with BACK STITCH.

9 outline in FRENCH KNOTS and vein with SATIN STITCH from mid-rib but not quite to outer edges

10 work in close FEATHER STITCH

11 Outline in CHAIN STITCH. For the centre, work mid-rib in STEM STITCH with BULLION STITCH branching out

12 work from mid-rib to outer edge in slightly padded BUTTONHOLE STITCH; work stem in STEM STITCH

Your finished sampler could be made into an oval or rectangular mat or you could frame it.

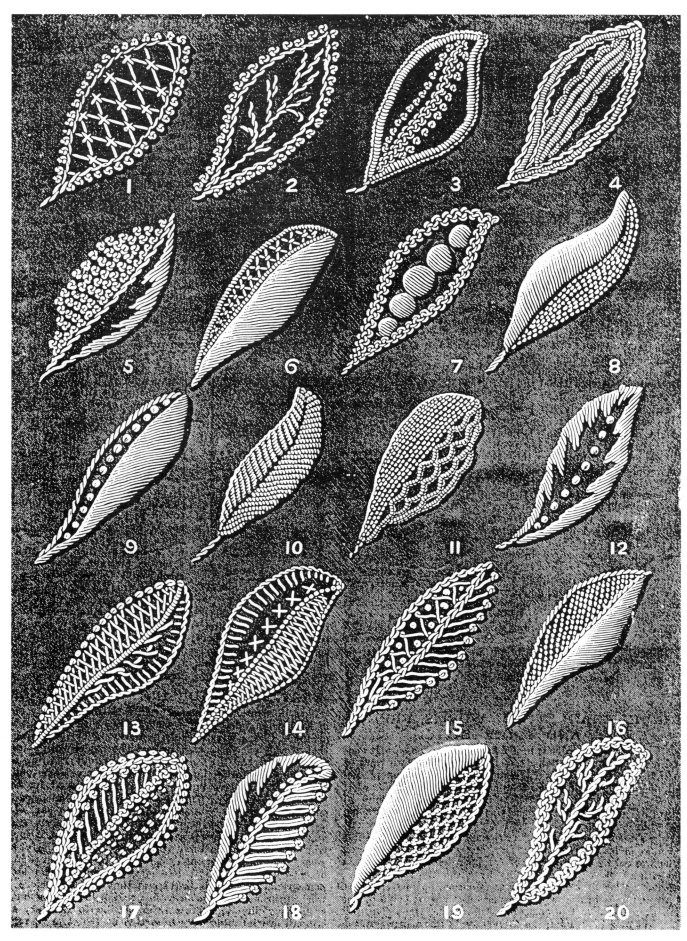

Sampler showing Twenty Leaves worked in the Newest Style of Mountmellick Embroidery.
From Weldon's *Practical Mountmellick Embroidery*.

Sampler showing Twenty Leaves

Leaf #1 – Leaf outlined in *crewel* stitch with an outer border of *French knots*. *Diamond filling* (long stitches caught at intersections with *cross stitches)*

Leaf # 2 – *Crewel stitch* outline and veinings. Outer border of *French knots*, slightly larger than on the first leaf. To make knots larger, do more wraps around needle.

Leaf # 3 – Leaf outlined in closely worked *padded buttonhole stitch*. Centre vein is in *cable plait* and on each side of the mid-vein is a row of *French knots*.

Leaf #4 – This leaf is a bit more complicated than the preceeding three. It is outlined in *padded overcast stitch*, with a row of *crewel* on either side. The centre vein is in *Point de reprise*, edged on either side with rows of *buttonhole loops*. Point de reprise: Take four long stitches the length of the leaf, like the strings of a violin; do not take the stitches through to the back, but keep the threads on the surface. Going under two threads and over two, etc. needle weave or darn over the stretched threads. Buttonhole loops: buttonhole stitches over loose threads, as in making button loops. The entire leaf requires careful, close stitchery.

Leaf #5 – One half of this leaf is worked in *French knots* clustered closely together. The centre vein is in *crewel* with the edge in slanting irregular *satin stitch*.

Leaf #6 – The centre vein and one half of this leaf are delineated in *padded overcast stitch*. Filling in *cross stitches* caught down with a small straight stitch. The other half is worked in *slanted satin* stitch.

Leaf #7 – This leaf is outlined in *cable plait* and filled with *satin stitched dots* of graduated size.

Leaf #8 – The left half of this leaf is worked in *padded satin stitch* and the right half in neat even rows of *back stitch*.

Leaf #9 – Right half is worked in *padded satin stitch*. The left half is outlined in *crewel stitch*. *Seed* filling.

Leaf #10 – Left half: *crewel* outline with *bullion stitch (worms)* filling. Right half: rows of crewel.

Leaf #11 – The left half of the leaf is outlined in *crewel* and filled with rows of *back stitch*. The right half is done in rows of *buttonhole loops*.

Leaf #12 – The leaf is embroidered in smooth *slanting overcast (satin) stitch*, with a filling of *seeds*.

Leaf #13 – Centre rib: *padded overcast* stitch. Left half of leaf: *seed* outline and *herringbone filling*. Right half: *crewel* outline with *straight stitch* filling.

Leaf #14 – Centre rib and right edge: *padded overcast* with *herringbone* filling. Left edge: *buttonhole* with *cross stitch* filling.

Leaf #15 – Centre rib and left edge: *Chainstitch*, with filling of *herringbone* and *French knots*. Right side of leaf: *couched long stitches* ending in French knots.

Leaf #16 – Centre rib and left edge: fine *crewel stitch*, with a filling of neat, small *back stitches*. Right edge: *padded satin stitch*.

Leaf #17 – This leaf is entirely outlined in *chain stitch*, with a row of *seed stitches* all round the outside. The mid-rib is in *French knots* and the *spike* (straight) stitches on the left side also end in French knots. Filling on right side: rows of seed stitch.

Leaf #18 – Mid-rib and left edge: *crewel* and *satin stitches*, with *seed stitch* just to left of rib. Right side of leaf: *spike stitch* and *French knots*.

Leaf #19 – The left side of this leaf is worked in well-padded *satin stitch*, and the right in *buttonhole filling* edged with *crewel stitch*.

Leaf # 20 – This last leaf is outlined in *cable plait* with mid-rib and veins of *crewel stitch*.

The Knitted Fringe

Although the example of Mountmellick work in the Victoria and Albert Museum has a lace trim, this is entirely uncharacteristic and the usual edging is the knitted fringe. This fringe is simple to knit and you may find it useful for other purposes as well. Use #13 or 14 knitting needles and the same cotton with which you embroidered. If you are using quite fine cotton, knit with 3 or 4 strands. Be sure to knit sufficient to go around your work plus a little extra for good measure!

Here are 3 methods of knitting the fringe, and one method of purling. Twelve stitches on the needle will produce a fringe 6″ wide. Use 1 to 4 strands from separate balls of thread.

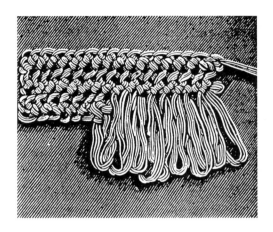

Method 1
Cast on 12 stitches (or any number divisible by 3)
First row: *Pass thread over the needle (y.o.), knit 2 together, knit one. Repeat 3 times to end of row.
Second row: Repeat from *
When you have knitted sufficient length, cast off 7 stitches, pass thread through last stitch. Unravel the last 4 stitches.

Method 2
Cast on 12 stitches
First row: *Knit one, yarn over (y.o.), knit 2 together. Repeat to end of row.
Second row: Repeat from *
With 12 stitches on needle, cast off 6 stitches. Cut thread and draw end through last stitch. Slip the last 6 stitches off the needle and unravel.

Method 3
Cast on 12 stitches.
First row: *Yarn over (y.o.), knit one, knit 2 together.
Second row: Repeat from *
Cast off 7 stitches and unravel the remaining 5.

Purled fringe
Cast on 9 stitches, using 3 strands from different balls.
1st row: Pass the cotton quite round the needle to make a stitch, purl 2 stitches together, purl 1; make one, purl 2 together, purl 1; make 1, purl 2 together, purl 1.
Every row is the same. When the length is done, cast off 5 stitches, draw the cotton through the stitch on the right-hand needle, and break it off and unravel the remaining stitches to form the fringe.

To Cast Off
Knit 2 stitches. *Pass the first stitch on the right-hand needle over the second stitch, leaving 1 stitch on the right-hand needle. Knit another stitch, again having 2 stitches on right-hand needle. Repeat from * until desired number of stitches is cast off.

Stitch the completed fringe to the buttonholed edge, using the same cotton.

Do NOT substitute crochet for knitting.

Do NOT clip the loops of the fringe.

Quilts and Clothing

'Those ladies who like making quilts in patchwork sections will enjoy the idea of preparing a number of squares measuring about 8″ each way, each square being embroidered with a different subject, and the whole sewn together and then prettily feather stitched over the seams; this might be quickly executed after the manner of a 'friendship quilt' by a number of friends joining in the enterprise and contributing 2 or 3 squares each . . . . '

Weldon's Third Series

A good idea and of course, the squares need not be that small! Traditional Mountmellick 'quilts' are really coverlets, in that they are neither padded nor lined. While retaining the character of Mountmellick work in the embroidery, it is perfectly possible to make a padded (wadded) quilt. Wash and iron the fabric as usual, and piece the quilt top to the desired size. Transfer the design to the quilt and embroider. (If very large, the quilt could be embroidered in sections and then put together.) Wash and iron the lining fabric – a fine cotton sateen is good for this. Sew the lining to the desired size. Assemble the quilt by making a 'sandwich' of the lining, 2 oz. polyester or cotton wadding, and the finished quilt top. Assemble the quilt by first pinning and then tacking (basting) to the corners and centre edges from the centre of the quilt, and then in a grid so that the quilt 'sandwich' is tacked every 5 or 6 inches. Mark for quilting, which can be done by 'powdering' with French knots or flower-like groups of bullion knots. The quilt can be lap or frame quilted. Avoid knots on the back of the work and instead, run the thread end through the layers and take a back stitch both for starting and finishing.

Because of all the layers, it is easier to bind such a quilt rather than use the knitted fringe. Cut a 2″ or 3″ binding from the cotton satin – the binding strips can be cut either on the straight or the bias. Pin and tack the finished binding to the front edges of the quilt, right side to right side. Machine sew, using a long stitch. Turn binding over the edge and to the back and slip stitch.

A label with your name and date of the work can be made for your quilt by cross-stitching over waste canvas onto a small piece of cotton satin and sewing the label to the back. The lettering can be worked out on graph paper before cross-stitching.

For clothing and other articles to be made up, it is easier to mark the embroidery designs on the fabric pieces, cut out, zig zag edges and complete the embroidery as much as possible before assembly. Be sure to use white thread when marking for darts, as coloured thread may 'bleed' on the fabric.

Ireland —   Maree Maher, 157 Templeogue Road, Terenure, Dublin 6W. Mail order for fabric (smaller amounts if wanted), starter packs, matt cotton threads in different weights, needles.

Needlecraft, 27 Dawson Street, Dublin 2. Mail order for fabric, thread, needles.

Britain —   Whaley's (Bradford) Ltd., Harris Court, Great Horton, Bradford, West Yorkshire BD7 4EQ. Whaley's weave the Heavy Cotton Satin, and will supply by mail order, minimum order 3 metres.

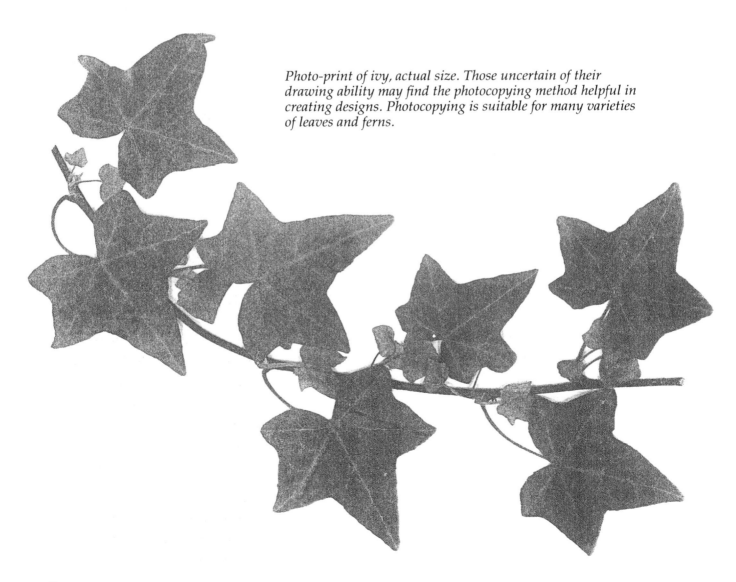

Photo-print of ivy, actual size. Those uncertain of their drawing ability may find the photocopying method helpful in creating designs. Photocopying is suitable for many varieties of leaves and ferns.

Part III: Mountmellick Work Pattern Sheets

The following patterns are copied from the original line patterns which have been preserved in various collections. These may be traced or copied to make full-size patterns from which the various motifs can be worked.

1. Dog Rose
2. Dog Rose
3. Hops
4. Bryony
5. Bryony
6. Dog Rose
7. Pimpernel
8. Fuchsia
9. Dog Rose and Fern
10. Blackberry
11. Pimpernel
12. Fern and Shamrock
13. Virginian Creeper
14. Bindweed
15. Stylised floral border
16. Daisy and Wheat
17. Virginian Creeper
18. Sweet Pea
19. Shamrock
20 and 21. Viola
22. Shamrock bouquet
23. White Beam
24 and 25. Dog Rose
26. Dog Rose and Forget-Me-Not
27. Cyclamen and Narcissus
28. Tiger Lily
29 and 30. Thistle
31. Daisy
32. Daisy and Shamrock
33. Blackberry
34. Blackberry
35. Clover
36. Passion Flower
37. Dog Rose
38. Ivy

39. Rowan and Fern
40. Oak
41. Maidenhair Fern
42. Elder
43. Tiger Lily
44. Initial 'S'
45. Centre spray with Honeysuckle, Forget-Me-Not and Dog Rose
46. Initial 'A'
47. Corner and borders of Virginian Creeper and Ivy
48. Shamrock wreath
49. Initial 'M' with Shamrock
50. Shamrock spray
51. Shamrock spray
52. Clover
53. Butterflies
54. Seashells and Seaweed
55. Honeysuckle and Dog Rose
56. Honeysuckle and Dog Rose
57. Shamrock and Dog Rose
58. Elder
59. Elder
60. Honey suckle and Dog Rose
61. Baby bib with Maidenhair Fern
62. Blackberry and Briar Rose
63. Initial 'K' with Shamrock
64. Initial 'A' with Forget-Me-Not
65. Word 'Letters'
66. Word 'Baby' with Shamrock
67. Corner spray with Passion Flower (half-scale)
68. Vine with Grapes (half-scale)
69. Sweet Briar spray (half-scale)
70. Alphabet (Union Pearl)

1. Dog Rose

2. Dog Rose

3. Hops

4. Bryony

5. Bryony

6. Dog Ros

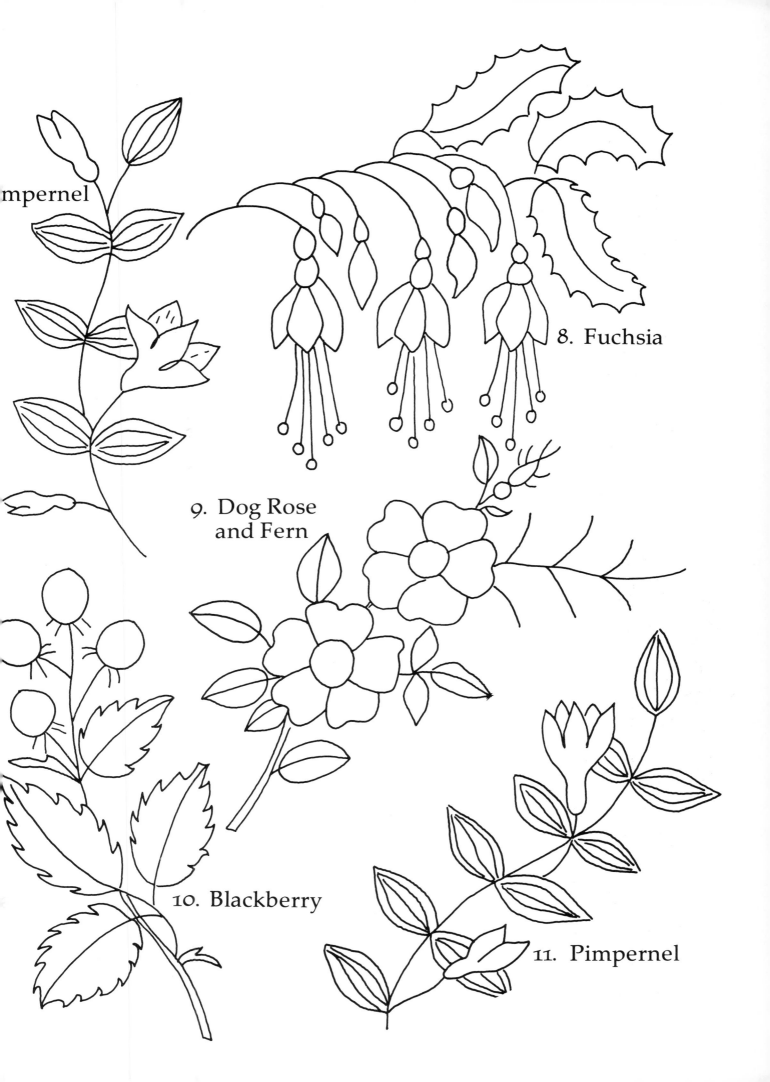

mpernel

8. Fuchsia

9. Dog Rose
and Fern

10. Blackberry

11. Pimpernel

12. Fern and Shamrock

1.

13. Virginian
Creeper

Bindweed

15. Stylised
floral border

16. Daisy and Wheat

17. Virg
Cree

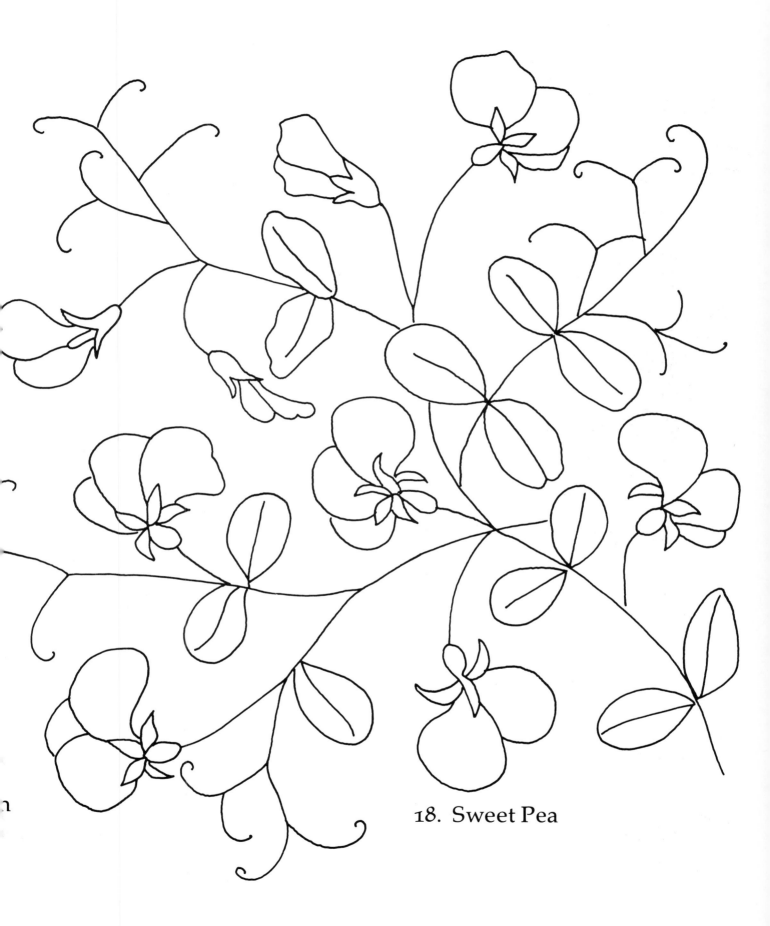

18. Sweet Pea

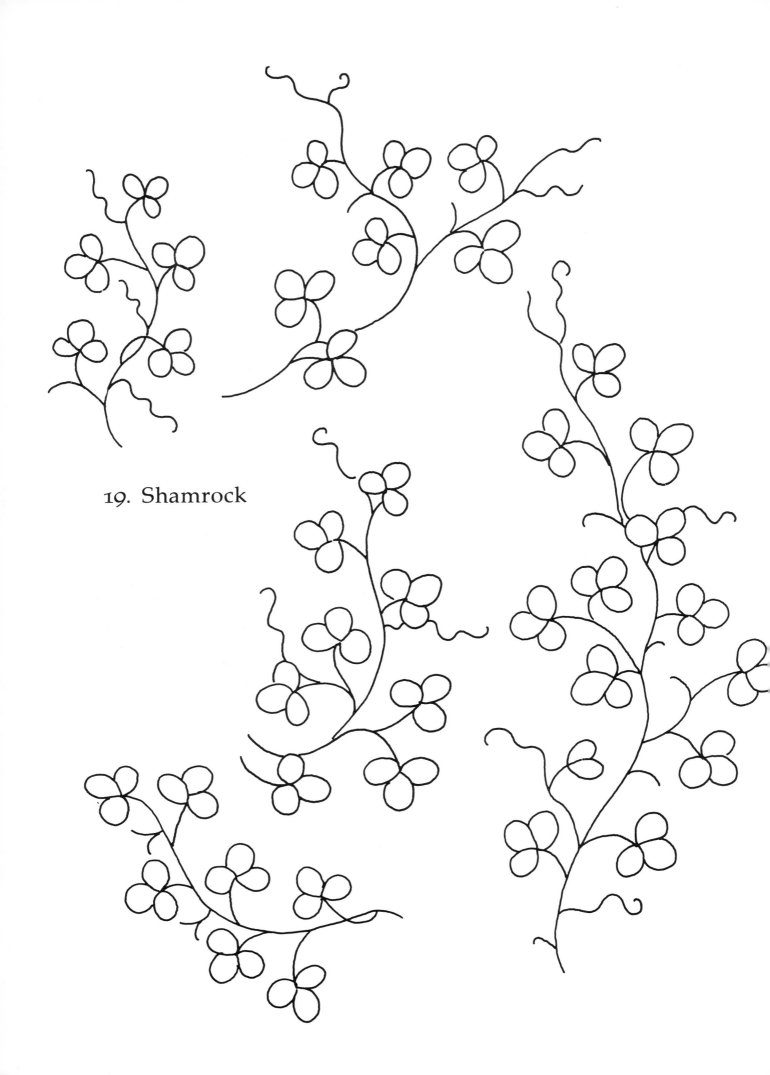

19. Shamrock

20 and 21. Viola

22. Shamrock bouquet

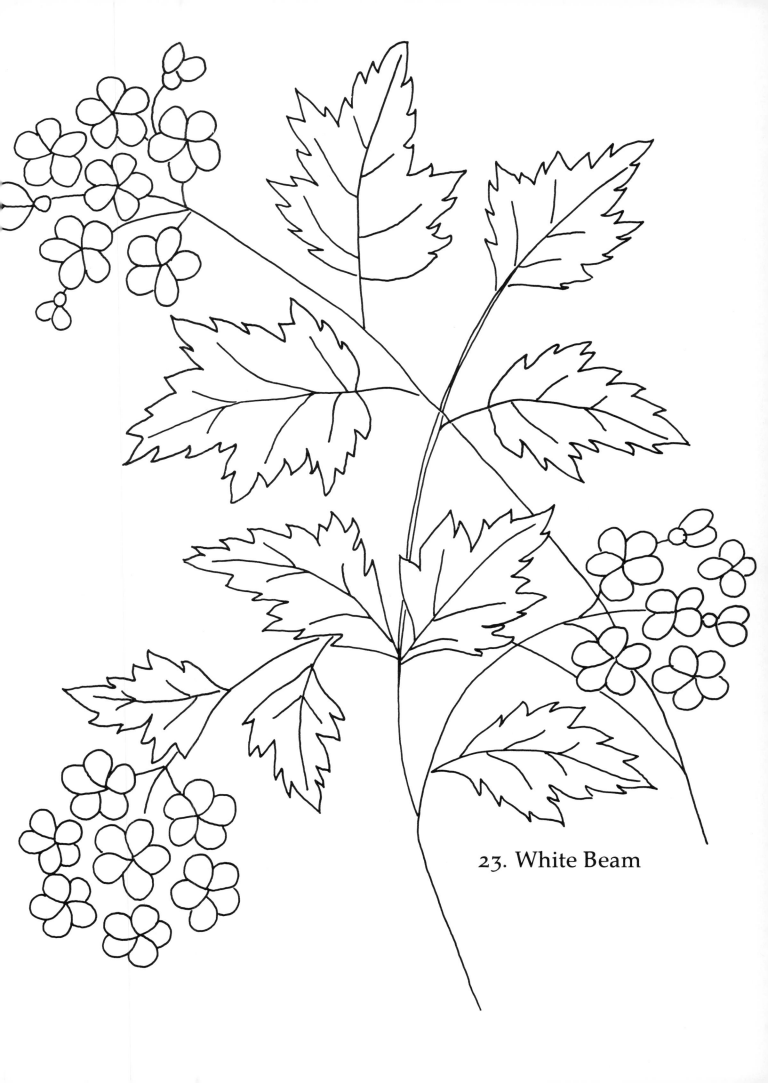

23. White Beam

24 and 25. Dog Rose

. Dog Rose and Forget-Me-Not

27. Cyclamen and Narcissus

28. Tiger Lily

29 and 30. Thistle

31. Daisy

32. Daisy and
Shamrock

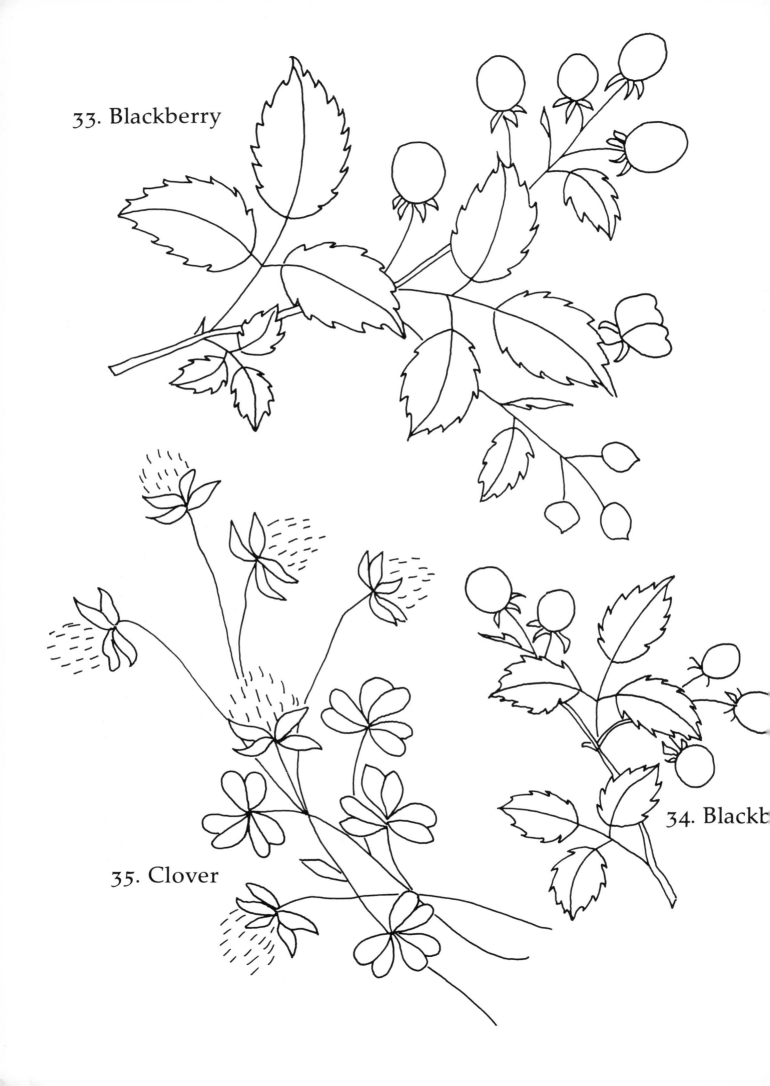

33. Blackberry

34. Blackb

35. Clover

37. Dog Rose

36. Passion Flower

38. Ivy

39. Rowan and
Fern

41. Maidenhair Fern

Oak

42. Elder

43. Tiger Lily

44. Initial 'S'

46. Initial 'A'

45. Centre spray with
Honeysuckle,
Forget-Me-Not and
Dog Rose

To extend the Virginian Creeper border, join a to a and b to b.

a

b

47. Co
borders
Creeper

a

b

and
irginian
Ivy

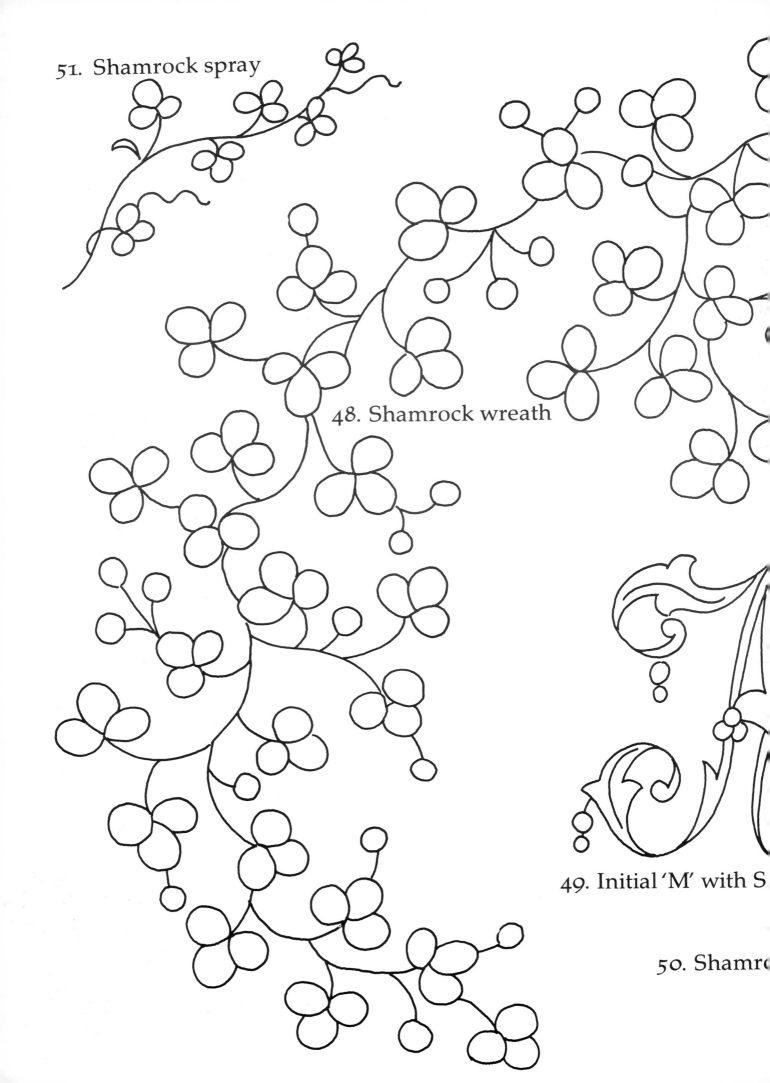

51. Shamrock spray

48. Shamrock wreath

49. Initial 'M' with S

50. Shamro

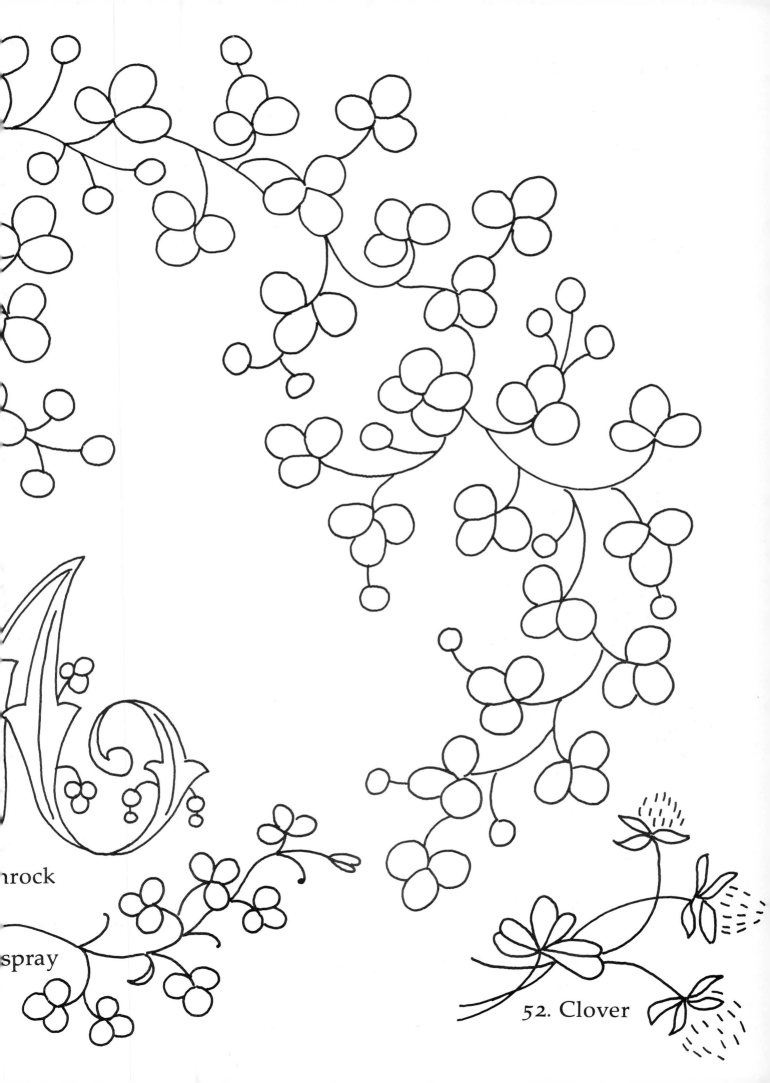

rock

spray

52. Clover

53. Butterflies

54. Seashells and Seaweed

55. Honeysuckle and
Dog Rose

56. Honeysuckle
and Dog Rose

57. Shamrock
and Dog Rose

58. Elder

59. Elder

60. Honeysuckle and Dog Rose

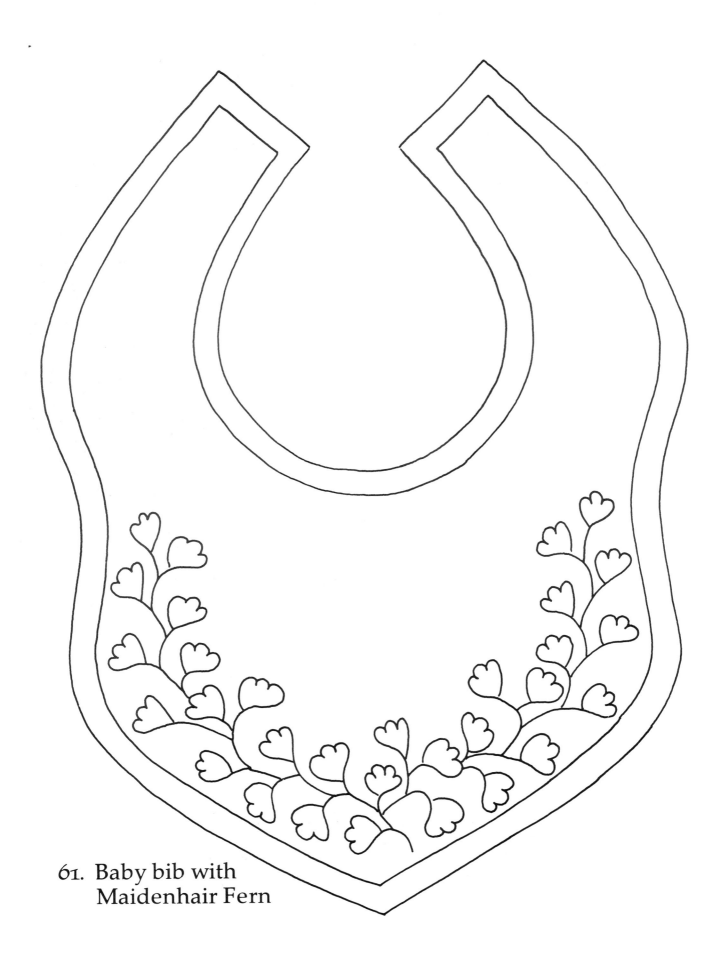

61. Baby bib with
Maidenhair Fern

62. Blackberry and Briar Rose

63. Initial 'K'
with Shamrock

64. Initial 'A' with
Forget-Me-Not

65. Word 'Letters'

66. Word 'Baby'
with Shamrock

68. Vine with Grapes

67. Corner sp
Passion Fl

The drawings on this sheet are half size. They may be brought up to size by using a copying machine which enlarges – or manually by making a grid of one-inch squares and re-drawing the designs.

69. Sweet Briar spray

70. Alphabet (Union Pearl)